AUG 9

LAUGHLIN

Birthdays

Paul Mason

Heinemann Library
Chicago, Illinois

Customer Service 888-454-2279
Visit our website at www.heinemannlibrary.com

Designed by David Poole and Geoff Ward
Originated by Ambassador Litho Ltd
Printed in China by Wing King Tong

08 07 06 05 04
10 9 8 7 6 5 4 3 2 1

Library of Congress Cataloging-in-Publication Data
Mason, Paul, 1967-
  Birthdays / Paul Mason.
      p. cm. -- (Rites of passage)
Summary: Explores the origin, historical significance, and practice of birthdays by different groups around the world and describes the various foods, rituals, and types of clothing associated with birthday celebrations.
Includes bibliographical references and index.
  ISBN 1-4034-3985-0 (lib. bdg.) -- ISBN 1-4034-4595-8 (pbk.)
  1. Birthdays--Juvenile literature. [1. Birthdays.] I. Title. II. Series.
  GT2430.M37 2003
  394.2--dc21
                          2003001894

Acknowledgments
The author and publisher are grateful to the following for permission to reproduce copyright material:
Cover photograph: Topham Picturepoint.
p. 4 Kevin Radford/Masterfile; pp. 5, 21 Peter Sanders; p. 6 Barbara Peacock/Corbis; p. 7 Catherine Ledner/Getty Images; p. 8 Dianna Sarto/Corbis; p. 9 Patrick Ward/Corbis; p. 10 Dallas and John Heaton/Corbis; p. 11 Michael S. Yamashita/Corbis; p. 12 Keren Su/Corbis; p. 13 Robert Harding; pp. 14, 28 Ariel Skelley/Corbis; p. 15 Uwe Krejci/ Getty Images; p. 16 Mary Evans Picture Library; p. 17 Getty Images; p. 18 Moshe Shai/Corbis; p. 20 Tiziana and Gianni Baldizzone/ Corbis; p. 22 Earl and Nazima Kowall/Corbis; p. 19 Richard Nowitz/Israelimages.com; p. 23 Phil & Val Emmett; pp. 24, 27 Alamy Images; p. 25 Ann & Bury Peerless; p. 26 Christine Osborne; p. 29 Trevor Creighton/Travel Ink.

Special thanks to Lynne Broadbent of the BFSS National Religious Education Center at Brunel University, England, for her help in the preparation of this book.

Some words are shown in bold, **like this.** You can find out what they mean by looking in the glossary.

Contents

What's in a Birthday?

There are many different kinds of birthday celebrations. The most common are people's own birthdays. People may throw a big party or just have a special meal with their family. Many people get presents and cards on their birthday.

"Happy Birthday to You"
The song many people around the world sing to wish someone a happy birthday was not originally a birthday song at all! It first appeared as "Good Morning to All," a **hymn** for school children to sing at the start of the day. It only became "Happy Birthday to You" in the 1920s or 1930s, about 30 years after it was written.

All around the world, birthdays are celebrated with special parties and games. The birthday girl or boy may also get presents.

Some birthdays have special meanings. One of the most important is the birthday that celebrates the change from being a child to being an adult. In most countries, this change happens when a person turns 18 or 21. There are other important birthdays as well. For example, in Japan, the ages of three, five, and seven years have special meaning.

These children are celebrating the birthday of the Prophet Muhammad.

Other birthdays are celebrated by large groups of people. Often, these celebrations are connected to a religion. For example, **Christians** celebrate Christmas, Jesus' birthday; **Muslims** celebrate the birthday of the **Prophet Muhammad.** Both are celebrations of important people of the religion, so they are very important to the religion's followers.

Rites of passage

In 1909, Arnold van Gennep wrote about rites of passage. He made up this term to mean events that mark important times in a person's life. He said there are three changes in every rite of passage:

- leaving one group,
- moving on to a new stage, and
- joining a new group.

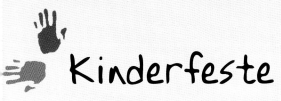

Kinderfeste

Many people believe that Germany is the place where children's birthday parties were first held. The German language even has a word for them—*kinderfeste* (kin-der-fess-tuh). The word *kinder* means small child, and the word *feste* means party or celebration.

This girl will get presents on her birthday because of ancient kinderfeste *customs.*

Kinderfeste became popular in Germany about 800 years ago. On the morning of a child's birthday, candles on a cake were lit. As the candles burned down they were replaced with new candles so that the candles burn all day. Then after dinner in the evening, the candles were blown out and the cake was finally eaten. The candles had to be blown out in one breath, and a wish was made. People believed that the wish would only come true if it was kept a secret. The birthday child was allowed to choose his or her favorite foods for dinner. The child was also given presents.

Kinderfeste customs today

Some customs from ancient *kinderfeste* survive today. Many children receive presents on their birthdays. Many also have cakes with lighted candles—and blowing out all of the candles at once still gives the birthday child a secret wish. In Germany, children are never given homework or chores on their birthday.

The Birthday Man

Traditionally, the Birthday Man appeared as part of *kinderfeste*. He was a bearded elf who brought presents to children who had been good. Up until the early 1900s, dolls of the Birthday Man could be found for sale, but he has now disappeared completely.

This child blows out candles on a birthday cake. Having candles on a birthday cake was part of the traditional kinderfeste *celebrations.*

Piñata Parties

Piñatas (pin-ya-ta) are popular in Mexico. A *piñata* is a brightly decorated container, often in the shape of an animal, filled with candy and small toys. In the past, *piñatas* were made of clay pottery. Today, most are made from **papier mâché**.

Hitting the piñata while blindfolded is hard. The job is made even harder by the fact that some people call out the wrong directions.

Piñata song

One of the songs people sing while someone is trying to hit a *piñata* goes:
"I don't want nickel, I don't want silver
I only want to break the *piñata*!"
The words come from the days of Spanish **colonialism.** In 1557, Spanish officials toured Mexico asking people to be loyal to Spain. In return, the people could trade cheap nickel coins for valuable silver ones.

On special occasions, such as birthdays and Christmas, a *piñata* is strung up so that it hangs from the ceiling. A blindfolded person tries to break the *piñata* open with a stick. People shout out directions. Some people shout wrong directions to try and fool the hitter into losing his or her turn. If the person is successful though, the *piñata* breaks open and spills its contents on the ground for everyone to share.

Quinceañera

In Latin America, a girl's fifteenth birthday is the day she becomes an adult. The celebration on this day, called a *quinceañera* (KWIN-say-a-NYAIR-a), often includes a religious **ceremony** at a church. Many *quinceañeras* include a candle-lighting ceremony. In some places, a young woman changes from flat shoes to high-heeled ones during the ceremony. This is a sign that she has grown up.

Shichi-go-san Festival

In Japan, a child's third, fifth, and seventh birthdays are thought to be especially lucky. A celebration is held each year on November 15 for children who have reached these ages during the last year. The celebration is called *Shichi-go-san* (shee-chee goh-san), which means "seven five three."

How it began

Shichi-go-san began many centuries ago. It marked important moments in a child's life. At three, boys and girls stopped having their heads shaved and were allowed to grow their hair. At five, boys stopped wearing babyish clothes and were allowed to wear *hakama* (ha-ka-ma—very wide-legged pants. At seven, girls were allowed to use an *obi* (oh-be), a kind of belt or sash, to tie their **kimono** (ki-mo-no) instead of a cord. *Shichi-go-san* is one of the important rites of passage of the **Shinto** religion.

People wearing traditional Japanese clothes gather for the Shichi-go-san festival in 2002.

These two girls are wearing kimonos, ready for their Shichi-go-san celebrations.

The modern festival

Families still celebrate *Shichi-go-san* today. They visit Shinto **shrines** and give thanks for being healthy. Afterward, many families have a celebration meal and give their child gifts. Children usually dress in their kimono or *hakama* for the **ceremony,** although some wear **Western**-style clothing instead. The family buys special candy called *chitose-ame,* which means "long-life sweets". These candies come in bags decorated with cranes—a type of bird—and turtles. Both are **symbols** of long life. The candies are given to relatives and neighbors when the family gets home from the shrine.

Matsuo's story

Matsuo Harada, now 11 years old, remembers *Shichi-go-san:*
I remember my last Shichi-go-san *really well. We went to the big shrine in Kagoshima, and my father rented a* hakama *for me to wear. There were lots of other children there too, all celebrating the festival.*

First Birthday

In many Asian countries, a child's first year is thought to be a special one. In the past, many children died during their first year. This sad fact may be why there are so many celebrations for one-year-olds.

China

When a Chinese child is one, there is usually a big celebration. One custom is for many different objects and toys to be put on the floor around a child—for example, pens, toy animals, and a model car. The item that a child picks up is supposed to give a clue about what he or she will do as an adult. For example, a child that picks up a pen might become a writer.

Tigers

In China, people think that tigers protect young children. New babies are always brought gifts of clothes or toys decorated with tigers. People hope that the tigers will help save their children from illness and bad luck.

This tiger is the kind of toy that might be given to a Chinese baby for luck.

Chinese families celebrate a first birthday with a special meal together. In Hong Kong, for example, people eat extra-long noodles at the birthday party. The long noodles are supposed to show that everyone wishes the birthday boy or girl a long life.

Korea

In Korea, a child's first birthday is also special, but another celebration comes first. *Paegil* (pay-gill) is the 100th day after a child's birth. It is a day of feasting for a child's family. *Paegil* dates back to the time when families celebrated the fact that their child had lived through a dangerous time and survived.

A Korean child's first birthday is called *tol.* Family and friends all come to the party and eat a big meal. The guests all offer the child money as a gift.

This Korean boy is celebrating tol, *his first birthday, which is why he is dressed in traditional clothes.*

Christmas

Christmas is one of the most important celebrations for **Christians.** They celebrate the day that Jesus, the son of God in Christianity, was born. Most Christians celebrate Christmas on December 25, but **Orthodox Christians** celebrate on January 7.

The Bible story

The **Bible** says that Jesus was born in a stable in a village called Bethlehem. His parents had traveled there to take part in a **census.** When they arrived, the only place for them to sleep was in a stable, among the donkeys and sheep. Jesus was visited there by shepherds who had been told by an angel to come. He was also visited by three wise men bearing gifts who had followed a star from the East.

Christmas today

Today, many parts of this story have found their way into Christmas celebrations. Many people give one another presents at Christmas, even if they do not go to church. This gift-giving reminds people of the gifts of the wise men. Homes may also have a Christmas tree with a star on top to remember the wise men. Or, a tree may have an angel on top in memory of the shepherds.

Children in a play recreate part of the story of Jesus' birth.

Children, along with adults, enjoy opening presents on Christmas Day.

Christians start to prepare for Christmas and Jesus' birthday during Advent. Advent begins on the Sunday closest to November 30. Christmas ends on the **Epiphany,** January 6, twelve days after Christmas Day. This is when families traditionally take down their Christmas decorations.

Many Christians go to church on Christmas Eve—December 24—to celebrate Jesus' birthday. There are also church services on Christmas Day. Later, people gather with their families and give each other presents.

Pierre's story

Pierre Villefranche, aged 14, describes Christmas in Belgium:

We give small family presents at Christmas. We put them under the tree or in stockings at night, to be found on Christmas Day. Christmas breakfast is cougnou, a kind of sweet bread in a shape that's meant to be like baby Jesus.

Christmas Customs

People celebrate Christmas in many different ways. Some
ways have connections to Jesus' birth—the angel or star on a
Christmas tree, for example. Other ways have their beginnings
in birthday celebrations around the world.

Giving presents

Giving presents is a common way of celebrating a birthday.
About two hundred years ago, in the 1800s, Saint Nicholas
became a popular **symbol** of gift-giving in many European
countries. He brought presents to children on the eve of
his **feast day.** Today, Saint Nicholas is often called Father
Christmas or Santa Claus.

*The first Christmas card was created by John Calcott Horsley in 1843. It looked
like a postcard and showed a large family enjoying a Christmas celebration.
The message read, "A Merry Christmas and a Happy New Year to You."
About 1,000 of the cards were sold.*

Decorations

People all around the world decorate their homes for birthday celebrations. At Christmas, many people have Christmas trees. Christmas trees were probably first used in Germany in the early 1600s. Before this, people had decorated a "Paradise Tree" as part of a popular play staged all over Germany on Christmas Eve. Over time, the custom of decorating a tree spread around the world.

The first Christmas trees had wafers hanging from them. The wafers stood for the body of Jesus Christ, whose birthday is celebrated at Christmas.

La Befana

In Italy La Befana (lah bef-ah-nah), a kindly, wrinkled old woman, brings presents on January 5, the night before the **Epiphany.** According to legend, the wise men asked her to come with them to see the infant Jesus. She refused, saying she was too busy and had to clean her house. So, she missed the wondrous sight. Each year La Befana goes from house to house, leaving gifts and looking for the baby Jesus.

Upsherin

Upsherin (upp-share-inn) is a haircut, but a very important one. In some **Jewish** families, boys do not have their hair cut until they are three years old. Then, it is cut during a **ceremony.** Friends and family are usually there. Sometimes long strands called *peyos* (pay-ohs) are left just above the ears. *Peyos* are worn because of a passage in the Torah, the Jewish **holy** book, that says hair should not be cut too short on the sides of the head.

Why wait three years?

A passage in the Torah says that the fruit of a tree should not be cut off and eaten for the tree's first three years. Some Jews believe that this means children's hair should also not be cut for the first three years of their lives.

This boy is about to have the first snips of hair taken off his head as part of his upsherin haircut.

What is special about *upsherin*?

Upsherin marks the moment when a baby becomes a child. After *upsherin*, a boy is allowed to wear items of clothing worn by adult men. For example, he can wear a *yarmulke* (yah-muh-kuh), a small cap worn on the top of the head. He also begins his religious training after *upsherin*.

Bar and bat mitzvah

Bar mitzvah is a Jewish celebration for boys and bat mitzvah is a celebration for girls. Jews mark the move from being a child to having the same duties as an adult. Bar and bat mitzvahs happen when boys are thirteen and when girls are twelve. The ceremonies involve the boy or girl reading the Torah in Hebrew in public to show that he or she is taking on an adult position.

This girl is reading from the Torah. It is a very important part of her bat mitzvah celebration.

The Birthday of the Prophet

The Birthday of the Prophet is an important celebration. It is held on the birthday of the **Prophet Muhammad,** the key figure of the **Muslim** religion. Not all Muslims celebrate it, however. In some countries, such as Saudi Arabia, the day passes by much like any other.

Where the Birthday of the Prophet is celebrated, like Egypt and Turkey, it is a happy time. Families come together to have a celebration meal. People spend money they have saved on candy, toys, clothes, and other treats.

These Muslims in Niger have gathered together to celebrate the Birthday of the Prophet.

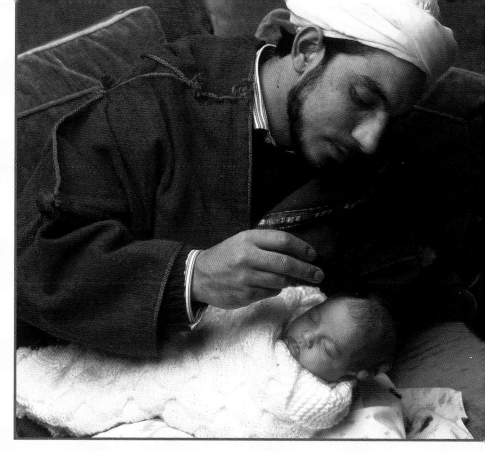

This Muslim man is very carefully shaving the head of his one-week-old baby.

People tell stories of the Prophet Muhammad, read poetry, and sing songs to praise him. There are also readings from the Qur'an (kor-AN), the Muslim **holy** book. Some families give food and money to the poor.

Many families visit a mosque, or Muslim place of worship, to hear a priest speak about the Prophet Muhammad. Loudspeakers allow those outside a mosque to hear.

Silver-haired babies

Wealthy Muslims may give thanks after a child is born by giving gifts to the poor. After a child is a week old, its head is shaved. The family then gives an amount of silver equal to the weight of the child's hair. Often extra silver is given, too. Afterward, family and friends meet for a feast where the child is named. Some of the food from the feast is also given to the poor.

Gurpurb

The **Sikh** religion is based on the teachings of ten great men, its first leaders. These leaders are called gurus, and their birthdays are among the most important events of the year for Sikhs. The celebration of a guru's birthday is called a *gurpurb* (gurr-purr-buh).

Guru Nanak's Birthday

Guru Nanak was the first guru of Sikhism. His *gurpurb* celebrations usually happen in the month of November. They begin two days before his actual birthday with a non-stop reading of the *Siri Guru Granth Sahib* (sir-ee goo-roo granth saa-hib), the Sikh **holy** book. One day before his birthday, a large **procession** is organized including religious leaders and ordinary worshippers.

These Sikh girls are wearing traditional clothes at the gurpurb for Guru Nanak in New Delhi, India.

Guru Nanak's birthday itself begins at 4 or 5 A.M., when the reading of the *Siri Guru Granth Sahib* has finished. There are special religious songs, readings from the *Siri Guru Granth Sahib,* and talks about the meaning of the Guru's words.

These activities go on until about 2 P.M. Then, people are given a sweet pudding called *karah parshad,* followed by a meal. This food is always eaten at the end of a service at a Sikh place of worship, or *gurdwara.* There can also be a night-time celebration, which ends at about 2 A.M. By that time, many people have been awake for about 22 hours!

Guru Nanak's birthday is celebrated each year by Sikhs. He is one of the founders of the Sikh religion.

Tegh's story

Tegh Singh, age eleven, from Lahore, India, describes a *gurpurb* for Guru Nanak Sahib:

The Guru was born very near to here, so we feel especially proud. People come from all over the world to visit the birthplace, and the procession through the streets of Lahore is a great colorful, noisy event.

Rama Navami

One of the great **Hindu** birthday celebrations is a nine-day festival called *Rama Navami* (rama nah-va-mee), in March or April. It leads up to the birthday of Rama, the human form of the Hindu god Vishnu. Rama's story is told in a long poem called the *Ramayana*. In it, Rama's wife Sita is kidnapped by a demon king named Ravana. Rama follows them. After many adventures, he kills the demon king with an arrow and saves Sita.

Hindu birthday traditions

On a Hindu child's first birthday, his or her head is shaved. Removing the hair is said to cleanse the child of any evil from past lives. It **symbolizes** a renewal of the soul. Hindu children only celebrate their birthdays until they are sixteen.

This Hindu boy is having his head shaved on his first birthday.

Celebrations

Rama Navami is especially important in the northern Indian city of Ayodhya, where Rama was born. A huge fair is organized for two days. Chariot **processions** leave from the temples, taking statues of Rama and Sita on tours through the city. The processions include people dressed in scenes from the *Ramayana*. Some people **fast** on the actual day of Rama's birthday.

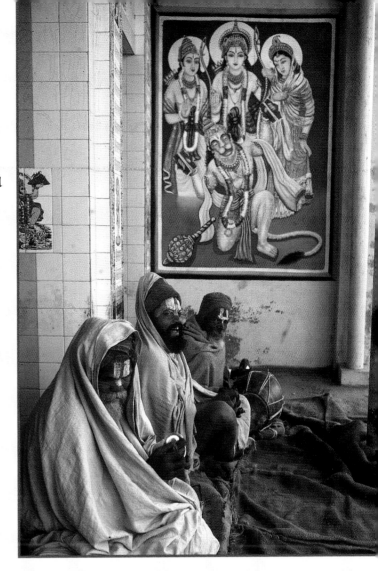

These people in India are celebrating Rama Navami, *the birthday of the man-god Rama. In the background is a picture of Rama, Sita, Hanuman, and Lakshman, characters from the* Ramayana.

Meera's story

Meera Shastri, nine years old, remembers *Rama Navami* in Jammu, India, in 2001:

This year the whole City of Temples was decorated with flags. The Maharani [wife of an Indian prince or ruler] came to visit the poor people and handed out 80 blankets and 10 sewing machines. My mother got one of the sewing machines!

Wesak

Wesak is the festival of Buddha's birthday. **Buddhists** believe that Buddha was a man who achieved enlightenment. Doing so meant Buddha had reached the highest state of spiritual or religious understanding possible. He was free from the cares of the world.

There are two main types of Buddhism. The first type is found in southeast Asia, such as Thailand and Laos. Its followers celebrate the birth, enlightenment, and death of Buddha all on the same day. This celebration occurs on the day of the first full moon in May. In a leap year, the festival is held in June. The second type of Buddhism is followed in central and east Asia, such as China, Japan, and Tibet.

These Wesak celebrations are taking place at a Buddhist temple in London, England.

Wesak celebrations may include visiting a temple to think about Buddha. Most Buddhists will decorate their houses with *Wesak* lanterns, oil lamps, and pandals. Pandals are bamboo canes covered in colored paper or cloth. Some Buddhists send *Wesak* cards to friends during the month of May.

Many lanterns have been used to decorate this house for Wesak *celebrations.*

Catherine's story

Catherine Ngo, now fifteen, describes *Wesak* celebrations in Vietnam:

> *I remember the* Wesak *celebrations from before we moved here to America, back in Vietnam. There are many Buddhists there, so lots of people celebrate Buddha's birthday. People would decorate their houses with lanterns and garlands [strings of flowers]. Some people set free caged birds, which stands for the compassion of Buddha.*

National Birthdays

In 1909, Arnold van Gennep said that a rite of passage involves three changes: leaving a group, moving on to a new stage, and joining a new group. Although he was talking about individuals, these changes can be applied to groups of people, even whole countries. When a country becomes independent, it goes through a rite of passage. In 1946, India was part of a group of countries that made up the **British Empire.** Then, on August 15, 1947, it moved on to a new stage and became an independent country. It joined a new group—the group of countries that make their own decisions and deal with their own problems.

The day on which a country becomes independent can be thought of as its birthday. People often have parties and celebrations on this day. The Fourth of July in the United States is the anniversary of the day when the country became independent—July 4, 1776.

These girls have dressed in patriotic clothing to enjoy Independence Day in the U.S.

These celebrations in Sydney Harbor were for Australia Day in 1998.

Today, many of the world's cities have large fireworks displays on their country's national birthday. There are often parades, games, concerts, speeches, and picnics. Some of the world's biggest national birthday celebrations are Australia Day (January 26), Bastille Day in France (July 14), and Independence Day in Mexico (September 16).

Year of Independence

The best year for Independence Days was 1960. Eighteen countries became independent: Somalia, Cyprus, Nigeria, Benin, Burkina Faso, Cameroon, the Central African Republic, Chad, Congo, Côte d'Ivoire, Gabon, Madagascar, Mali, Mauritania, Niger, Senegal, Togo, and Zaire.

Glossary

Bible Christian holy book

British Empire parts of the world that were ruled by Great Britain, mainly during the 1800s and 1900s. It covered much of the world, including large parts of the Caribbean, Africa, and India.

Buddhist person who follows the way of life taught by Buddha, who lived in ancient India about 2,500 years ago. Buddha was not a god, but a man. He taught his followers how to live simple, peaceful lives, called Buddhism.

census survey taken to gather information about the number of people living in a specific area, their jobs, their ages, and other details about their lives

ceremony special ritual or celebration

Christian person who follows the religion of Christianity, which is based on the teachings of Jesus Christ. Christians believe that Jesus was the son of God.

colonialism process of taking over and ruling another country, making it a colony. For example, when Spain ruled Mexico, it was a Spanish colony.

compassion feelings for another's hardship that leads people to be helpful or kind to others

Epiphany day of the appearance of the wise men to visit the baby Jesus, which Christians celebrate on January 6

fast go without food

feast day religious event that celebrates an event or honors a god, person, or thing

Hindu person who follows Hinduism. Hindus worship one god, called Brahman, in many forms. Hinduism is the main religion in India.

holy special, because it has to do with God or a religious purpose

hymn song in the praise of God

Jew person who follows the religion of Judaism. Jews pray to one god.

kimono traditional Japanese robe, often made of silk

Muslim person who follows the religion of Islam. Muslims pray to one God, whom they call Allah.

Orthodox Christian member of a branch of Christianity that developed separately from the Roman Catholic Church. Roman Catholicism developed in the West, Orthodox Christianity in the East.

papier mâché strong material made of newspaper and glue that hardens after drying

procession people walking together along a route as part of a public or religious festival

Prophet Muhammad key person of the Muslim religion

Shinto ancient Japanese religion in which nature is very important

shrine place of worship that is linked with someone who has died, for example a saint

Sikh person who follows the religion of Sikhism, based on the teachings of the ten gurus, or teachers

symbol when a picture or object stands for something else

Western something from Europe, North America, or Australasia or from those cultures

More Books to Read

Dineen, Jacqueline. *Births.* Chicago: Raintree, 2001.

Marchant, Karena. *Muslim Festivals.* Chicago: Raintree, 2001.

Spirn, Michele. *Birth.* Farmington Hills, Mich.: Blackbirch Press, 1998.

Wallace, Paula S. *The World of Birthdays.* Milwaukee: Gareth Stevens, 2003.

Index